CAMPING
BASICS

HOW TO SET UP CAMP, BUILD A FIRE, AND ENJOY THE OUTDOORS

Johnny Molloy

T0166305

Adventure Skills Guides

GET OUTDOORS AND CONNECT WITH NATURE

Adventure Skills Guides

The difference between a good camping trip and a not-so-good camping trip is having the skills that give you an edge—from pitching your tent in the correct spot or staying dry during a thunderstorm to stoking an inviting fire. Quality camping skills will help you deal with bugs, rain, and other outdoor unpleasantries.

Camping skills help you smooth out the edges, taking the rough out of roughing it. Then you can better enjoy the experience for which you came, soaking in the sunshine with friends and family, spending quality time together in the great outdoors, and enjoying a respite from the daily grind. Quality camping skills create the best outdoor event possible. This guide will teach you those skills.

JOHNNY MOLLOY

Johnny Molloy is an outdoor writer who has camped more than 4,500 nights in his lifetime and in locales ranging from Alaska to Florida. He has authored over 75 outdoor guides and continues to enjoy camping, backpacking, hiking, and paddling throughout North America. Johnny lives in Johnson City, Tennessee.

Cover and book design by Jonathan Norberg
Edited by Brett Ortler

Cover image: **James Aloysius Mahan V/Shutterstock.com**

All photos by Johnny Molloy unless otherwise noted.
All images copyrighted.

Used under license from Shutterstock.com:
Alfa Photostudio: 12 main, 24 main; **aSuruwataRi:** 9b; **Brent Hofacker:** 23 main; **Brett Holmes:** 12a; **Bruce Ng:** 13b; **chuchai jaiboon:** 21 main; **Daniel Krason:** 16 main; **Daxiao Productions:** 6 main, **encierro:** 18 main; **FootMade0525:** 6a; **Jan Faulkner:** 13a; **Jaromir Chalabala:** 7a; **Jasmine Sahin:** 10 main; **Matthew E. Hein:** 4a; **MPH Photos:** 15b; **New Africa:** 23a; **nikitabuida:** 9a; **Phill Danze:** 7b; **PhotoSky:** 3 main; **Predrag Milosavljevic:** 21a; **Roger Brown Photography:** 19 main; **samulisnre:** 10a; **Sean Thomforde:** 24a; **simoly:** 8a; **Techa Boribalburipun:** 22 main; **Virrage Images:** 8 main; **vladimir salman:** 14a; **XiXinXing:** 25 main; **Yurasov Valery:** 11a

10 9 8 7 6 5 4 3 2

Camping Basics: How to Set Up Camp, Build a Fire, and Enjoy the Outdoors
Copyright © 2021 by Johnny Molloy
Published by Adventure Publications, an imprint of AdventureKEEN
310 Garfield Street South, Cambridge, Minnesota 55008
(800) 678-7006
www.adventurepublications.net
All rights reserved
Printed in China
ISBN 978-1-64755-032-5

When planning a camping trip, consider group dynamics before you leave.

Group dynamics are critical. Personality conflicts can be more damaging to a camping trip than other problems, such as bad weather. When assembling a group, deliberate whether individual members will get along and cooperate. Also factor in demeanor, toughness, and political and religious outlook among other traits.

Next assess group size and trip expectations. The more people, the more complicated things become. Once the camping party is assembled, review trip practicalities such as exactly where, when, and for how long you are camping. Also review gear, especially gear that is shared by the group.

Arrive at a consensus about the length and style of the trip. Does everyone want to hike, bike, and paddle all day long and spend little time at camp? Or do they want to spend more time relaxing by the fire? Families often make a good group because they know each other's strengths and weaknesses. However, camping newbies can be another story. If taking a newbie camping, plan the trip with them in mind. Consider their physical abilities and inexperience when choosing where to camp and what to do—after all you want them to like it. Factor in weather. A first-timer is not going to enjoy spending the whole day getting soaked. Pick a good weather window.

Don't intimidate. Initiating your friend is not an opportunity to show what a great camper you are—that you can set up a tent in three minutes—it's about the new camper and their experience.

No matter your group composition, make it clear up front about sharing expenses, chores, and other duties. This way there will be no unpleasant surprises when it comes time to collect money—or firewood. After all parties come to agreement about the adventure, review the details one last time, then you're ready to go!

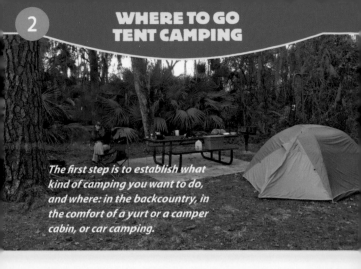

The first step is to establish what kind of camping you want to do, and where: in the backcountry, in the comfort of a yurt or a camper cabin, or car camping.

First decide what type of camping you want to do. Do you want to camp in the frontcountry, places accessible by vehicle? Or do you want to head to the backcountry, usually accessible by foot, but also by canoe, kayak, or bicycle? Most of us will be frontcountry camping, or car camping as it is known. First, seek out state and national parks as well as state and national forests if adding nature-based activities such as hiking, paddling, and nature study to your camping agenda. These parks preserve special scenic and natural areas, and often include campgrounds, allowing you to pitch your tent amid nature's splendor and enjoy nature-based activities near the campground.

Seek private campgrounds when location is important (if you want to camp near a theme park or concert site, for example.) Fees will generally be higher at private campgrounds, and they often are geared more toward RV campers than tent campers. Select a private campground if you want increased amenities such as on-site laundry, game rooms, and more luxurious bathhouses.

Ramp up your camping game by renting a yurt or camper cabin, often including decks and furniture. Yurts are a combination of cabin on the bottom and fabric on top, often circular, but with other variants. Your chosen state park or private campground may offer yurts or camper cabins for rental. They're unusual, fun, and associated with "glamping," aka glamorous camping.

Choose backcountry camping if you like to keep it simple. Most backpacking camps are a designated spot with a fire ring, occasionally with a picnic table and outhouse. Other backcountry campsites, such as those in national forests, are just traditionally camped-upon flat spots, not official designated campsites, usually with water access. Backcountry campers should bring everything they need. Reservations can be made for backcountry sites at some state and national parks.

Be sure to make reservations in advance when car camping, especially on busy holiday weekends. Many online reservation platforms show photos of each campsite, though the pictures are not always helpful, given the lack of perspective. If you arrive at the campground and your site is unfavorable, ask to switch—it can't hurt. Once at a favored camping destination, peruse the campground and take note of your favorite campsites. That way in the future you can reserve the site that best suits you.

When camping, preparation is key, and a little organization and planning ahead will make the trip a lot easier.

When camping, preparation saves more time and trouble than it consumes. Keep your camping gear stored in one place, in a dry area using labeled storage bins. Before packing, consider your camping company, weather, and potential activities while camping. Use the camping checklist in this guide or make your own and store it on your phone, then use the list every time you pack, continually tweaking it.

Gear Keep your tent in its storage bag with all contents inside, from tent fly to stakes to groundsheet. The same goes for sleeping bags, sleeping pads, and camping pillows. Keep cooking gear stored together. Other items such as tarps, trekking poles, packs, and fishing gear can be considered on a trip-by-trip basis.

Lighting Be prepared for nighttime. Have headlamps, flashlights, and lanterns all charged and/or with fresh batteries.

Food The best way to prepare your food is to make a list of meals for your trip. For example, Friday: dinner, Saturday: breakfast, lunch, dinner, Sunday: breakfast, lunch. Add snacks and drinks, then determine what foods—and supplies to cook them—are needed for each meal. Enter the list on your phone, then shop.

Cooler To keep your cooler cold as long as possible, pre-chill it with ice before adding ice for your camping trip. Keep the cooler in the shade, out of a hot car, and away from the fire. Minimize opening and closing it. Drain the cooler in the morning and evening to keep food from floating.

But the best thing you can do is line your cooler with dry ice—frozen carbon dioxide, -109.3°F cold. For best dry ice results, pre-chill the cooler with water ice then line the cooler bottom with dry ice. Next put regular ice atop the dry ice. Store your goodies inside and away you go.

Clothing If car camping, bring enough clothing for all potential weather conditions you anticipate—and then some, if rain is expected. Remember your rain jacket, too. Hats provide cooling shade and layering warmth. They also cover "bedhead" for that morning trip to the campground bathhouse. A spare pair of socks helps for cold nights and in case your trip is a little wetter than anticipated. Bandanas are all-purpose—they keep your head/neck warm, cover skin, and can be used as a wash rag. Backcountry campers should consider the weight of clothing and only bring the bare minimum of essentials.

Toiletries Have a separate camping toiletries kit, or use your travel toiletries kit. Use travel-size toothpaste, shampoo, and other necessities to save space. Be even more determined to downsize your toiletry kit when backcountry camping.

To save time, shop and prepare a day or two before your camping adventure, including fueling up your vehicle. Once at camp you'll be able to enjoy yourself instead of making a food or supply run.

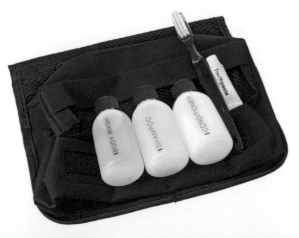

When buying a tent, don't scrimp. You definitely get what you pay for.

Tents are the time-honored shelter of choice for campers. Tents perform five primary functions: keep the bugs out, protect you from rain, make it a little warmer, block the wind, and deliver privacy. Tents also provide mental protection when night falls and young or inexperienced campers begin imagining wild animals and goblins lurking in the dark.

Tents are governed by the adage "You get what you pay for." Don't scrimp on a tent. When purchasing a tent select an established brand. Choose a tent with a built-in vestibule. That way you can keep your shoes/pack protected from precipitation yet not inside the tent.

Calculate how many people will be sleeping in the tent. If the answer is two then look for a 3–4 person tent. If you are sleeping four, then look for a 6–8 person tent, and so on. Tent manufacturers like to brag on how many a tent sleeps, but going by their guidelines you'll be sleeping like sardines. Big families can use multi-room tents, but finding the perfect spot to pitch them can be exceedingly difficult. Instead, go for two or more tents, allowing better tent site placement. Additionally, you can use smaller tents separately if your camping group size decreases.

Use a groundsheet or included footprint under the tent. It keeps the tent cleaner, drier, and extends the tent's life. Make sure the groundsheet is not exposed outside the tent or rain will pond on the groundsheet then run under the tent.

Backcountry campers require a smaller tent, sacrificing tent space for less weight. Be prepared for a tight squeeze when sharing a backpacking tent. Consider a tarp for shelter if not in bug country.

SLEEPING BAGS, PADS, AND MATTRESSES

Create your best chance for a good night's rest by putting together the whole package of the correct tent, sleeping bag, pillow, and sleeping pad.

Having the proper sleeping bag can mean the difference between a good night's rest and a miserable night followed by exhaustion the next day. When choosing a sleeping bag, the primary concerns for campers are warmth, space, and weight. Match your sleeping bag to the season and situation.

For all but the warmest times I recommend a full length zippered sleeping bag that is comfort rated to around 40°F. These can handle local cold fronts in spring and fall, as well as summer nights in the mountains without weighing too much. If it warms up, unzip the bag and use it as a blanket. In winter and in colder places consider a zero-degree bag. It will have thick baffling and an insulated hood among other features that will keep you warm and toasty. In warm summertime conditions use a simple fleece blanket—an item you can get cheaply.

For additional comfort consider carrying a small camp pillow, either fabric or an inflatable variety. Don't underestimate the importance of a pillow.

Sleeping pads are every bit as critical to a good night's rest as a sleeping bag and pillow. Pads range from closed cell foam pads to inflatable mattresses replicating a king-size bed. Backcountry users can bring lighter model air mattresses that weigh about a pound. Beware sleeping on an air pad in frigid weather; the air inside the pad cools down, and then it cools your body. Hammock campers need to add extra warm padding during cold spells.

Waterside campsites are always a hit. Choose one with a view if you can get it.

A campsite requires two things: A flat spot and access to water. Beyond those two necessities, assess the natural characteristics of the land to help you deal with the situation at hand. Seek an open, breezy location if the insects are troublesome. Find a sheltered location if the winds are howling. Seek shade if it is hot, or camp near ample fallen wood for a fire if it is cold. Utilizing natural attributes will keep you more comfortable in camp.

When setting up the tent try to find level ground that is not subject to water flow from uphill. Scan the ground where you plan to sleep for evidence of water running through that spot. If so, find another location. Also look for a layer of natural duff, such as leaves or pine needles, which indicates water doesn't run through the site; running water scours the ground. Duff also pads your bedroom. Do not clear the ground before setting up your tent, but do remove sticks, rocks, and other obstructions that might interrupt your sleep. Hammock campers simply need two conveniently located trees.

Most parks have specific developed sites that campers have to use—many with gravel for improved drainage—but even when perusing a campground with designated sites, look for the above characteristics—mostly level, dry ground that will drain if needed. Other considerations at developed campgrounds include site privacy, site spaciousness, quiet, and security.

Privacy lovers should seek natural borders between campsites, allowing everyone their personal space. Bigger families and groups should look for larger sites with room to spread out. Solitude lovers strive for the sounds of nature. Consider your camping neighbors and their "noise potential" before choosing your site.

Campground security is relative. A remote campground in an undeveloped area is usually safe, but don't tempt potential thieves by leaving your valuables out for all to see. Use common sense, and go with your instinct. Campground hosts are wonderful to have around, and parks with locked gates are ideal for security. Visit your neighbors and develop a buddy system to watch each other's belongings when possible.

Raising the bar, seek other characteristics that make your campsite not only functionally desirable but also aesthetically appealing. Waterside campsites are always a hit. Choose a site with a view if you can get it.

Assess campsite safety. Look for widow makers—dead standing trees or large hanging branches that may fall during a storm. Flooding is also a potential threat. Don't choose a campsite or set your camp close to water if heavy rains are in the forecast.

Backcountry campers should consider "camp furniture." At previously established backcountry sites, look for a combination of logs and rocks centered on a fire ring, creating benches and tables on which to place gear. Developed campgrounds likely will have a picnic table, allowing you to dry your gear.

Campfires are a storied tradition and they can serve a number of purposes.

A campfire has three main purposes: aesthetic appeal, cooking, and heating. Therefore when establishing your fire, determine its purpose. Most fires will involve two or more purposes. But first, you need wood.

Gathering wood After setting up camp—whether in the frontcountry or backcountry—the first thing to do is gather wood. Consider purchasing wood from the campground when possible. It is locally sourced; additionally, some state parks don't allow wood gathering. Don't transport wood from your home to a distant campsite; it could be harboring invasive insects or other pests.

When gathering wood use the following tactics: If you are at a heavily used site look for the most difficult terrain, such as a steep hill or ultra-dense forest and head straight that way to retrieve firewood. The easiest places to access will have been combed over already, so go to the more difficult places first. Secondly, go a fair distance from the campsite, say 60 to 80 yards. No matter where you are, there is a perimeter where campers cease wood hunting. At river or beach campsites, look along the water's edge for driftwood. No matter how you gather it, the wood will warm you three times: while gathering it, while breaking it up, and while burning it.

Campfire Safety This involves monitoring a fire from beginning to end. First, check in advance about fire restrictions, especially during spring and fall fire season, as well as dry periods. Be careful when breaking apart wood, especially using an ax or hatchet. The tools can get into the wrong hands—read: kids—with disastrous results. Don't jump on a limb to break it in two, you may break your ankle instead. Once your fire is started, watch it at all times. Extinguish it upon leaving. (For steps on how to safely build, and then put out a fire, see the fold-out portion of this guide.)

Keep kids, pets, and the tent away from the fire. Clear the area around the fire ring, especially at night, to avoid tripping into the flames. Beware picking up partially burned wood pieces; they may be burning on their unseen side. Watch for burning steam blowing out of ends of limbs. Heed popping coals that can land on your clothes—and your person.

Campfire cookery is an art and a camping tradition to embrace.

Cooking up tasty foods is a camping tradition whether you cook over the fire or a camp stove. Camp stoves are more efficient and easily regulated. Cooking over a fire can be difficult, as the cook must potentially contend with a heat source that can be smoky, too hot, or not hot enough, not to mention blackened pots and burned fingers. Stoves are less subject to rain and wind. But you must bring adequate fuel.

Yet campfire cookery is an art and a camping tradition to embrace. When campfire cooking, use already established fire rings, whether they are piled stones or park-provided steel grates. Have adequate wood ready before you start cooking.

Have your food/cooking utensils and spices ready to cook at the same time as the coals. Bring a lightweight grate, so you can place it wherever needed to best take advantage of the heat. Flames and coals wax and wane, therefore adjust your grill closer or farther from the heat as needed. If boiling water, use flames to heat the water, as opposed to coals, which are better for grilling and frying.

Stoves: Camping stoves range from massive multi-burners to tiny alcohol stoves. White gas stoves and butane cartridge stoves are the most popular. Single-burner white gas stoves with a built-in gas tank are best. They are in one piece, thus more portable and durable. Liquefied gas stoves use cartridges. Once opened, the cartridges leave you wondering exactly how much fuel is in them, necessitating having to carry an extra cartridge. Also, cartridge disposal is problematic. Large groups can use two-burner white gas stoves. Use alcohol stoves in the backcountry when weight is an issue. They deliver a weak, noncontrollable flame, but they are adequate for boiling water.

Cooking Safety: Use a cooking mitt when handling hot items. Be aware of the kids when you're using sharp knives, marshmallow sticks, hot grills, and while boiling water.

Food Storage: In the frontcountry, store your food in your car, which is a requirement in most bear-country campgrounds. This will also help you defend it against other lovers of human food—mice, raccoons, crows—and your own pet. In summer, food spoilage can be an issue. Put your food away before it goes bad.

In the backcountry some established campsites have bearproof lockers or storage cables. If you aren't that lucky, bring 50 feet of thin yet strong cord and hang your food. To do so, hang the bag from an outstretched limb that is at least 14 feet above the ground, 4 feet below the limb and 6 feet away from the trunk of the tree. It takes practice, so do it before dark and seek out a suitable tree well before attempting. For further safety measures consider cooking well away from your sleeping area.

Treat your water obtained from the backcountry.

Bring your own water or use treated sources whenever possible, such as at developed campgrounds. Your next option is using water from local sources, such as lakes, though you need to consider if the water source could be polluted from old mines, excessive farmland runoff, or other situations.

So what can drinking bad water do? Microbes such as giardia and *Cryptosporidium* get in your intestines and disrupt your life with excessive gas, diarrhea, and other unpleasantries. Giardiasis—the illness caused by giardia—won't ruin your average camping trip, as it takes 1 to 2 weeks for symptoms to appear. But once symptoms crop up expect to be ill for 2 to 6 weeks.

My first water-treatment choice is a simple filter such as one from Sawyer. It is lightweight, cheap, and lasts for years. It has special microbe-blocking membranes and operates using gravity—or squeeze pressure if in a hurry. Buying a water bottle with a built-in filter is an easy choice. Simply fill your water bottle then suck through a straw. UV filters are another option; they use ultraviolet rays to kill the bad things in the aqua. These products, such as Steripen, require batteries.

Chemical water treatments work, too. Products like Aqua Mira require you to mix two drops of chemicals, making chlorine dioxide, in untreated water, and wait 30 minutes, then your water is fine. You can always boil water if no other options are available. Boil untreated water for at least a minute. If you're at higher elevations (more than 6,500 feet), boil it for at least three minutes.

Give all wild creatures a wide berth.

BLACK BEARS AND GRIZZLY BEARS

When camping, a part of us wants to see a black bear or other wild creatures. But seeing one near your camp or at close-range is another thing altogether. If you are at camp and encounter a bear at close range, stay calm, stay standing upright, and avoid direct eye contact. Slowly back up—do not turn and run. The bear's instinct for the chase may leave it chasing you.

Give the black bear a clear escape route, then yell, bang pots, and make loud noises, encouraging the bruin to leave. Start slowly backing into your vehicle or some structure if you feel the need. In the meantime put away any vulnerable food. Don't throw the bruin food as a distraction.

Carry bear spray with you if you're in grizzly country, but don't use it upon first seeing a bear. It may go away on its own. Wait until the bear gets close enough for an effective shot (easier said than done). Hike and camp in groups of 4 or more if possible. If attacked by a grizzly, play dead, lying face down with your hands covering the back of your neck.

RACCOONS

Unless rabid, raccoons pose little danger. A rabid raccoon behaves almost as if drunk, swaying as it walks and looking confused. Get away and notify local authorities.

SNAKES

Consider yourself lucky if you see a snake. These reptiles are generally more wary of people than people are of snakes. Keep your distance and don't fool with a snake for any reason. If you see a snake sunning on the trail, simply give it a wide berth.

Always bring repellent in case biting bugs are a problem.

Clothing is your first line of defense against biting insects, including mosquitoes, gnats, yellow flies, common black flies, and no-see-ums. Starting at your feet, wear full shoes, thick socks, and long pants, even if the temperatures are warm. Your clothes should be thick enough to ward off a bite.

A long-sleeve shirt and a bandana around your neck come next. This leaves your head and hands exposed and is where bug spray comes in. I recommend chemical repellent, with DEET. Citrus-based and other natural repellents offer limited effectiveness. Bring repellents with differing amounts of DEET to suit the "skeeter meter," from 5 percent DEET to 40 percent or more; use only the amount of DEET you need. Consider spraying repellent directly on your socks or onto a bandana then tying it around your neck. When applying repellent to your face, spray it onto your hands then rub onto your face, avoiding your eyes. Wash your hands after applying repellent. Plan your application around eating and drinking. If things get really bad consider a head net. When selecting a campsite with bugs in mind, find campsites facing the wind. Then place your tent door into the breeze, keeping mosquitoes from congregating at the door during your entry and exit. Avoid being outside your tent during dusk and dawn. Wear light-colored clothing; bugs are attracted to dark clothing.

A real danger is from bee stings; anyone allergic should carry an Epipen. Campers should carry Benadryl-based creams to soothe bites from insects.

TICKS

Ticks need a host to reproduce, and we've all heard of Lyme disease, so prevention is key. Wear long pants and tuck them inside your socks, then spray with DEET-based bug spray. Permethrin works, too. Spray it on your clothes (not skin). It kills on contact. Check yourself and children daily. Ticks that haven't attached are easy to remove, hard to kill. If you find one on you, smush it or throw it in the fire. Use tweezers to remove embedded ticks.

For weather safety bring a portable weather radio with 24/7/365 broadcasts, alerting you to potentially life-threatening weather.

Campers live out in the weather and the seasons. Knowing the weather is invaluable when camping. You can bring gear and clothing appropriate for the situation, or you can call off your trip altogether.

A smartphone is a good first option for obtaining weather info. With your phone you can view not only predicted weather, but also real-time radar, hourly, and even minute-by-minute forecasts, as well as weather watches and warnings issued by the National Oceanic and Atmospheric Administration (NOAA). When it comes to weather, knowledge is not only power—but safety.

But don't depend on a phone as your only source of information, as reception is almost always a concern in the backcountry. For that reason, consider bringing a portable weather radio with 24/7/365 weather broadcasts from NOAA. NOAA not only predicts forthcoming weather, but it also gives short-term forecasts, alerting you to potentially life-threatening storms as they spring up. For those camping near the ocean, NOAA also offers marine forecasts, including wind speed and direction, as well as tide tables.

No matter what, check the weather before leaving home, including average highs, lows, and precipitation to help you prepare for your camping trip. In extreme weather—heat, cold, rain, or snow— your attitude is the most important thing you can control. Keeping a positive frame of mind can not only make the situation more tolerable, it can also help you make sound decisions if weather conditions become dangerous. Secondly, quality matters—good tents, tarps, raingear, jackets, boots, and socks can be the difference between staying warm and dry or cold and wet.

Bring a portable solar panel to charge your smartphone.

Even though camping seems decidedly low-tech (often on purpose), technology has filtered into the camping world. Your smartphone can be a camping wonder tool. Assuming you have service, it can function as a weather station, walkie-talkie, GPS, field guide, flashlight, star finder, and more.

Bring the phone along but also be sure to have charging capabilities. Many frontcountry campgrounds have electricity at each site. There's also your vehicle for charging, but be careful not to run the car battery down. It's surprisingly easy to do, so bring jumper cables just in case. Remember your charger cord, as well as an adapter for your car and for a standard electric plug. Backcountry campers can include small portable power packs that can recharge your phone numerous times. Store your phone in a waterproof case or at least a ziplock bag.

Solar chargers will keep your electronics running, from phones to anything that needs rechargeable batteries. Most camping solar chargers either roll or fold up for maximum portability. Your smart phone can enhance your camping trip; just don't make it the focal point of your campout. We use our phones enough at home and on the job.

Hygiene is as important when camping as it is as home.

Campers should be clean for both their own benefit and for their camping neighbors. Always use available restrooms in campgrounds and wash your hands afterwards. Be a good steward of public restrooms whether you are using the toilet, sink, or showers. Bring hand wipes as well as toilet paper.

Keep a clean campsite as well. Store items when not in use. Wind and rain can blow loose trash and clothes all over the campground. Put away food if it is not being eaten. It will attract everything from ants to bears.

Conditions can be a little more challenging in the backcountry. Not only should you consider other campers around and those who come after you but also the environment. Don't pollute water sources with bad hygiene. When nature calls dig a hole at least 100 feet from water and about 6 inches deep. Do your business, burn your toilet paper, then bury the evidence, sparing both the environment and the next camper unsightly, unsanitary hygiene practices.

Camping is a social activity, even if you don't always see your neighbors, so practice good camping etiquette.

Before you go camping, obtain all permits and authorization as required. Pay designated fees even if no one else is around. If camping permits require using the Internet, get your permit before entering iffy reception zones.

Camp in open destinations both in the frontcountry and backcountry. Respect closures. There's usually a valid reason if a camping area, trail, or destination is closed—storm damage, a bridge out, wildlife breeding area, and so on.

Pack out what you pack in—and more. No one likes to see the trash someone else has left behind.

Preserve the resource. Great care and money have gone into creating the campgrounds and parks. Don't deface signs, trees, or stack rocks. There's no need to let passersby know you were here.

Never spook wildlife. An unannounced approach, a sudden movement, or a loud noise startles most animals. A surprised animal can be dangerous to you, to others, and to themselves. Give them plenty of space.

Honor leash laws. Most campgrounds require your dog being on a 6-foot leash. Think of your fellow campers before setting your dog free. Unleashed dogs will also chase wildlife and perhaps become hurt or lost.

Plan ahead. Know your equipment, your ability, and the area where you are camping, then prepare accordingly. Be as self-sufficient as possible. A potential rescue is costly and can endanger the rescuers themselves.

Finally, be courteous to other campers and outdoor enthusiasts. After all, we are enjoying the same slice of nature together. Let's make it better for each of us in turn. A little etiquette at camp can go a long way to smooth things out when we're roughing it.

One way to get kids to love camping is simple: Don't forget the s'mores.

You want your child to love camping as much as you do. Getting them involved in each aspect of the adventure is a great way to keep them engaged, from loading the vehicle and pitching the tent to campfire cookery to stretching out the sleeping bags at bedtime.

Involvement starts at home. Get their input on camp foods and activities before arrival. Once at camp, give them tasks and work together. It's a real way to interact: the younger the child the easier the task. Let them set out the tent stakes or put mustard on the hot dog buns, even if they don't do it perfectly. It gives them a sense of accomplishment. Expect to work on their time, not on grownup time. Be patient.

Engage in outdoor activities that interest them. Don't forget the camping traditions. They're traditions for a reason. Cook s'mores, tell ghost stories around the campfire, and make shadow puppets in front of the flashlight. Have fun!

Build in rest time. Kids aren't going to pace themselves as adults will. When they run out of energy, let them conk out, even if it doesn't suit your timing.

Bring along noncamping pursuits. Allow a time for gaming or playing with toys, in addition to outdoor activities. That way they won't perceive camping as a denial of things, and they may surprise you by going full-out for the outdoor life.

Before you leave on your trip, be honest: If your dog isn't well-suited for camping, find a dog sitter.

First, make a candid assessment: Is your dog a camping dog? Leave an inside dog inside. If your dog can camp then bring it on. As with human campers preparation is key.

Bring dog food, leash, toys, and chews, a towel for dirty paws, and some type of bed. Determine whether or not your dog is going to sleep in the tent. If not, consider putting the dog bed under a tarp or consider bringing a pen. While at camp make sure your dog has varied sun and/or shade according to the weather conditions.

Be ready to control your dog when other campers come near. Keep it on a leash out of consideration for other campers, other dogs, and wild animals that dogs will likely chase. Dogs will get territorial with your campsite, perhaps growling at passersby. It's a dog's natural instinct, but you need to curb that while at a campground. And remember, always clean up after your dog.

Try to include the dog in activities where possible—hiking is always a good choice. Riding in a canoe, kayak, or swimming is fun, too. After all, dogs aren't called man's best friend for nothing.

Taking care of your gear and stowing it away after each trip will make your next one much easier!

Not only is it good practice to take care of your camping equipment during your campout, but it saves gear, time, and money to properly stow it away for your next outdoor adventure. First, dry out your tent, even if you didn't get rained on. Dew can have enough moisture to damage a packed-away tent. Set up the tent and fly at home in the sun if possible, and let it fully dry out. Sweep out debris such as sand, and leaves.

Air out your sleeping bags, letting them dry, too. Store them open, not cinched up in a stuff sack. This allows the sleeping bag fill to stay lofty. Unroll sleeping pads and dry them on both sides.

Wash your cups, utensils, and cook kits at home. It might be a while before you go camping again, and you'll appreciate the clean utensils next go round. Empty daypacks and backpacks, making sure they aren't harboring an apple or half-eaten candy bar, rendering them disgusting next time you use them. Air and dry the packs as well.

Hang coats and rain jackets on a hanger to air and dry. Throw your dirty camping clothes in the hamper, then you're done. All this might sound like a hassle but you will protect your camping gear and won't end up with a moldy tent next time you head off on a camping adventure.

TENT CAMPING CHECKLIST

Tents, Sleeping Bags, Pads, and Pillows

Tent with rain fly

Tent groundsheet/ footprint

Adequate sleeping bags

Sleeping pads

Air mattress/ electric pump

Camp pillows

Cooking and Food Storage

Cooler

Water container

Water filter

Pots/frying pans

Grill

Stove

Stove fuel

Cups

Knives/forks/spoons

Spatula/long spoon/ other utensils

Scrub brush/ dish soap

Spices/sugar/syrup

Cooking oil

Multiple lighters

Firestarter

Can opener

Corkscrew

Foil

Paper towels/napkins

Other Gear

Camp chairs

Headlamp/ flashlight/lantern

Spare batteries/ battery charger

Rope

Clothing

Long-sleeve shirts

Short-sleeve shirts

T-shirts

Long pants

Short pants

Socks

Bathing suit

Bandana

Ball cap/sun hat/ rain hat

Down jacket

Rain jacket/pants

Sandals

Hiking shoes/boots

Water shoes

Personal

Phone/charger/ cord/plug/ waterproof case

Solar charger

Toothbrush/ toothpaste/floss

First aid kit/ Band-Aids/ Benadryl cream

Pain reliever

Insect repellent

Sunscreen/lip balm

Bath soap/ washcloth/towel

Lotion

Toilet paper/ hand wipes

Sunglasses with neck strap

Water bottle

Other Helpful Gear

Weather radio

Maps as needed

Fishing rod/ reel/tackle

Hiking poles

Canoe/kayak/ paddles/life vests

Books

Camping with Kids

Kid specific clothing/gear

Games/toys

Camping with your Dog

Dog food/treats

Leash

Dog toys/towel

Dog bed/pen

After Your Camping Trip

Air out tent

Air out sleeping bags

Unroll pads/ mattresses

Wash camp dishes/ pots/utensils

Empty backpacks/ daypacks

Hang coats/jackets to dry

Store gear after drying